This Journal belongs to:

_____

_____

_____

Why should you use this
Prayer Journal ?

Because you are the child of God, and your care is essential to him. You should try to understand yourself and your feelings and align them with God's teachings.

Because God will never leave your side, so it is important to thank him for his everlasting love.

Because you should choose the right path to follow in life, and God will always guide you.

So, speak up for what you believe in, write your thoughts, spread God's word, and be a good example for your peers.

Do what you set your mind to, as God will give you strength and answer to your prayers.

"But to all
who did receive him,
who believed in his name,
he gave the right
to become children of God."
John 1:12

to aknowledge _____

I feel

😀 🙂 😐 🙁 ☹️

The best part of my day

_____
_____
_____
_____
_____
_____
_____
_____

My worries

_____
_____
_____
_____
_____

to write

Dear God, ♡

I am thankful for

_____

_____

_____

_____

_____

_____

_____

_____

I am praying for

_____

_____

_____

_____

_____

_____

_____

_____

to do

Today I learned a lot and I will practice

_____

_____

_____

_____

Thank you, God, for listening to me!

to doodle

Amen

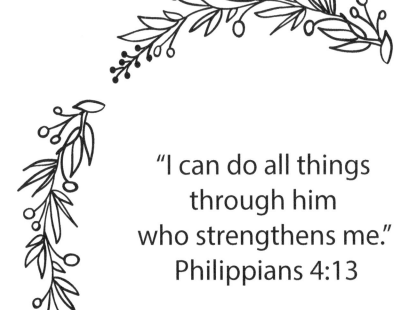

"I can do all things
through him
who strengthens me."
Philippians 4:13

to aknowledge

I feel

😃 😊 😐 ☹️ 😦

The best part of my day

_____
_____
_____
_____
_____
_____
_____
_____

My worries

_____
_____
_____
_____
_____

to write

Dear God, ♡

I am thankful for

_____
_____
_____
_____
_____
_____
_____
_____

I am praying for

_____
_____
_____
_____
_____
_____
_____

to do

Today I learned a lot and I will practice

_____

_____

_____

_____

Thank you, God, for listening to me!

to doodle

Amen

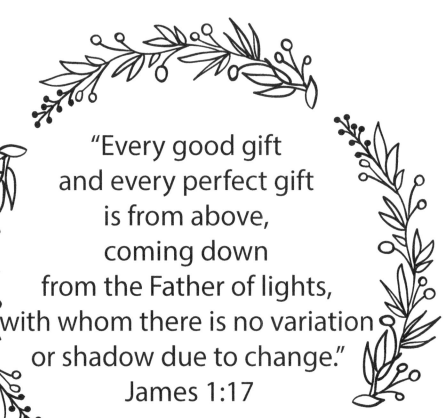

"Every good gift
and every perfect gift
is from above,
coming down
from the Father of lights,
with whom there is no variation
or shadow due to change."
James 1:17

to aknowledge

I feel

The best part of my day

_____
_____
_____
_____
_____
_____
_____
_____

My worries

_____
_____
_____
_____
_____

to write

Dear God, ♡

I am thankful for

_____

_____

_____

_____

_____

_____

_____

_____

I am praying for

_____

_____

_____

_____

_____

_____

_____

_____

to do

Today I learned a lot and I will practice

_____

_____

_____

_____

Thank you, God, for listening to me!

to doodle

Amen

"Say to those
who have an anxious heart,
"Be strong; fear not!
Behold, your God will come
with vengeance,
with the recompense of God.
He will come and save you.""
Isaiah 35:4

to akriowledge _____

I feel

😀 🙂 😐 🙁 ☹️

The best part of my day

_____
_____
_____
_____
_____
_____
_____

My worries

_____
_____
_____
_____

to write

Dear God, ♡

I am thankful for

_____
_____
_____
_____
_____
_____
_____
_____

I am praying for

_____
_____
_____
_____
_____
_____
_____
_____

to do

Today I learned a lot and I will practice

_____

_____

_____

_____

_____

Thank you, God, for listening to me!

to doodle

Amen

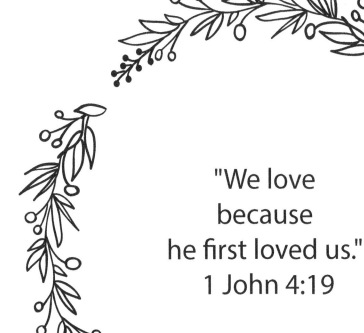

"We love
because
he first loved us."
1 John 4:19

to aknowledge

I feel

The best part of my day

My worries

Dear God, ♡

I am thankful for

_____
_____
_____
_____
_____
_____
_____
_____
_____

I am praying for

_____
_____
_____
_____
_____
_____
_____
_____
_____

to do

Today I learned a lot and I will practice

_____

_____

_____

_____

_____

Thank you, God, for listening to me!

to doodle

Amen

"but Jesus said,
"Let the little children
come to me
and do not hinder them,
for to such belongs
the kingdom of heaven.""
Matthew 19:14

to aknowledge

I feel

☺ ☺ 😐 ☹ ☹

The best part of my day

_____
_____
_____
_____
_____
_____
_____

My worries

_____
_____
_____
_____

to write

Dear God, ♡

I am thankful for

_____
_____
_____
_____
_____
_____
_____
_____
_____

I am praying for

_____
_____
_____
_____
_____
_____
_____
_____
_____

to do

Today I learned a lot and I will practice

_____

_____

_____

_____

Thank you, God, for listening to me!

to doodle

Amen

"When I am afraid,
I put my trust
in you."
Psalm 56:3

to aknowledge

I feel

The best part of my day

_____
_____
_____
_____
_____
_____
_____
_____

My worries

_____
_____
_____
_____
_____

to write

Dear God, ♡

I am thankful for

_____
_____
_____
_____
_____
_____
_____
_____
_____

I am praying for

_____
_____
_____
_____
_____
_____
_____
_____
_____

to do

Today I learned a lot and I will practice

_____

_____

_____

_____

Thank you, God, for listening to me!

to doodle

Amen

"fear not,
for I am with you;
be not dismayed,
for I am your God;
I will strengthen you,
I will help you,
I will uphold you with
my righteous right hand."
Isaiah 41:10

to aknowledge

I feel

😀 🙂 😐 🙁 ☹️

The best part of my day

_____
_____
_____
_____
_____
_____
_____

My worries

_____
_____
_____
_____

Dear God, ♡

I am thankful for

_____
_____
_____
_____
_____
_____
_____
_____
_____

I am praying for

_____
_____
_____
_____
_____
_____
_____
_____
_____

to do

Today I learned a lot and I will practice

_____

_____

_____

_____

Thank you, God, for listening to me!

to doodle

Amen

"Let everything
that has breath
praise the LORD!
Praise the LORD!"
Psalm 150:6

to aknowledge

I feel

The best part of my day

_____
_____
_____
_____
_____
_____
_____
_____

My worries

_____
_____
_____
_____
_____

to write

Dear God, ♡

I am thankful for

_____
_____
_____
_____
_____
_____
_____
_____

I am praying for

_____
_____
_____
_____
_____
_____
_____
_____
_____

to do

Today I learned a lot and I will practice

_____

_____

_____

_____

_____

Thank you, God, for listening to me!

to doodle

Amen

to read

"The Lord is my light
and my salvation;
whom shall I fear?
The Lord is the stronghold
of my life;
of whom shall I be afraid?"
Psalm 27:1

to aknowledge

I feel

The best part of my day

_____
_____
_____
_____
_____
_____
_____
_____

My worries

_____
_____
_____
_____

to write

Dear God, ♡

I am thankful for

_____
_____
_____
_____
_____
_____
_____

I am praying for

_____
_____
_____
_____
_____
_____
_____

to do

Today I learned a lot and I will practice

_____

_____

_____

_____

_____

Thank you, God, for listening to me!

to doodle

Amen

"Set your minds on things
that are above,
not on things
that are on earth."
Colossians 3:2

to aknowledge

I feel

The best part of my day

_____

_____

_____

_____

_____

_____

_____

My worries

_____

_____

_____

_____

to write

Dear God, ♡

I am thankful for

_____
_____
_____
_____
_____
_____
_____
_____

I am praying for

_____
_____
_____
_____
_____
_____
_____
_____

to do

Today I learned a lot and I will practice

_____

_____

_____

_____

_____

Thank you, God, for listening to me!

to doodle

Amen

"For where your treasure is,
there will your heart
be also."
Luke 12:34

to aknowledge   _____

I feel

The best part of my day

_____
_____
_____
_____
_____
_____
_____
_____

My worries

_____
_____
_____
_____

to write

Dear God, ♡

I am thankful for

_____
_____
_____
_____
_____
_____
_____
_____

I am praying for

_____
_____
_____
_____
_____
_____
_____
_____

to do

Today I learned a lot and I will practice

_____

_____

_____

_____

_____

Thank you, God, for listening to me!

to doodle

Amen

to read

"The fear of man
lays a snare,
but whoever trusts in the LORD
is safe."
Proverbs 29:25

to aknowledge _____

I feel

The best part of my day

_____
_____
_____
_____
_____
_____
_____

My worries

_____
_____
_____
_____

to write

Dear God, ♡

I am thankful for

_____
_____
_____
_____
_____
_____
_____

I am praying for

_____
_____
_____
_____
_____
_____
_____

to do

Today I learned a lot and I will practice

_____

_____

_____

_____

_____

Thank you, God, for listening to me!

to doodle

Amen

"The LORD is good to all,
and his mercy is over all
that he has made."
Psalm 145:9

to aknowledge

I feel

😀 🙂 😐 🙁 ☹️

The best part of my day

_____
_____
_____
_____
_____
_____
_____

My worries

_____
_____
_____
_____

to write

Dear God, ♡

I am thankful for

_____
_____
_____
_____
_____
_____
_____
_____

I am praying for

_____
_____
_____
_____
_____
_____
_____
_____
_____

to do

Today I learned a lot and I will practice

_____

_____

_____

_____

_____

Thank you, God, for listening to me!

to doodle

Amen

"Let the word of Christ
dwell in you richly,
teaching and admonishing
one another in all wisdom,
singing psalms
and hymns and spiritual songs,
with thankfulness in your hearts
to God."
Colossians 3:16

to aknowledge _____

I feel

The best part of my day

_____
_____
_____
_____
_____
_____
_____
_____

My worries

_____
_____
_____
_____

Dear God, ♡

I am thankful for

_____

_____

_____

_____

_____

_____

_____

I am praying for

_____

_____

_____

_____

_____

_____

_____

to do

Today I learned a lot and I will practice

_____

_____

_____

_____

Thank you, God, for listening to me!

to doodle

Amen

"God is our refuge
and strength,
a very present help
in trouble."
Psalm 46:1

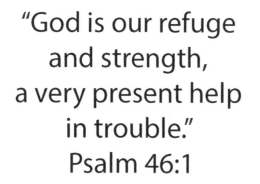

to aknowledge

I feel

The best part of my day

_____
_____
_____
_____
_____
_____
_____

My worries

_____
_____
_____
_____

to write

Dear God, ♡

I am thankful for

_____
_____
_____
_____
_____
_____
_____
_____

I am praying for

_____
_____
_____
_____
_____
_____
_____
_____
_____

to do

Today I learned a lot and I will practice

_____

_____

_____

_____

_____

Thank you, God, for listening to me!

to doodle

Amen

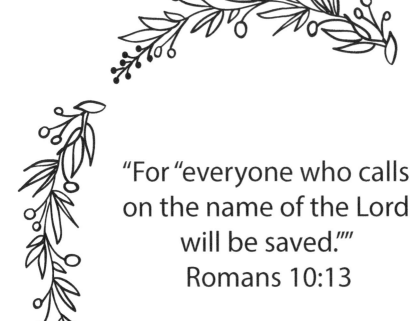

"For "everyone who calls
on the name of the Lord
will be saved.""
Romans 10:13

to aknowledge _____

I feel

The best part of my day

_____
_____
_____
_____
_____
_____
_____
_____

My worries

_____
_____
_____
_____

to write

Dear God, ♡

I am thankful for

_____
_____
_____
_____
_____
_____
_____
_____

I am praying for

_____
_____
_____
_____
_____
_____
_____
_____

to do

Today I learned a lot and I will practice

_____

_____

_____

_____

_____

Thank you, God, for listening to me!

to doodle

Amen

to read

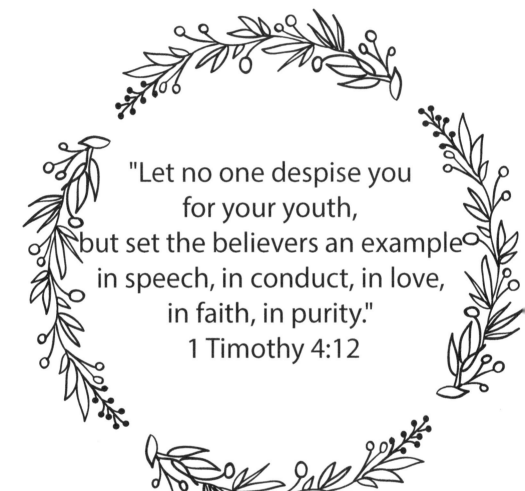

"Let no one despise you
for your youth,
but set the believers an example
in speech, in conduct, in love,
in faith, in purity."
1 Timothy 4:12

to aknowledge

I feel

The best part of my day

My worries

to write

Dear God, ♡

I am thankful for

_____
_____
_____
_____
_____
_____
_____
_____

I am praying for

_____
_____
_____
_____
_____
_____
_____

to do

Today I learned a lot and I will practice

_____

_____

_____

_____

_____

Thank you, God, for listening to me!

to doodle

Amen

"Keep your heart with
all vigilance, for from it
flow the springs of life."
Proverbs 4:23

to aknowledge

I feel

The best part of my day

_____

_____

_____

_____

_____

_____

_____

My worries

_____

_____

_____

_____

to write

Dear God, ♡

I am thankful for

_____
_____
_____
_____
_____
_____
_____
_____

I am praying for

_____
_____
_____
_____
_____
_____
_____
_____
_____

to do

Today I learned a lot and I will practice

_____

_____

_____

_____

_____

Thank you, God, for listening to me!

to doodle

Amen

to read

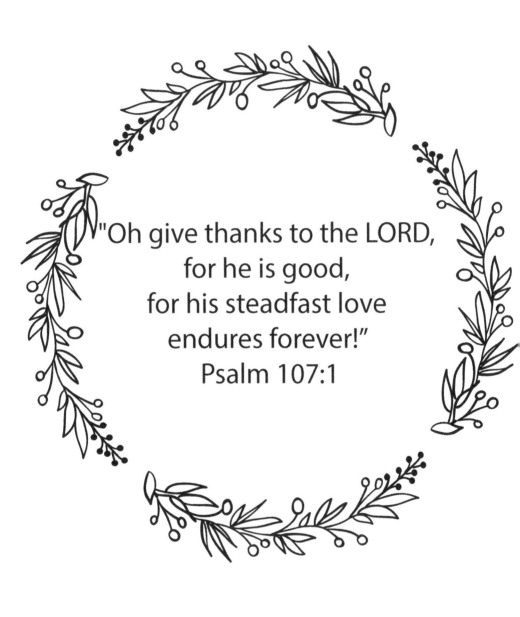

"Oh give thanks to the LORD,
for he is good,
for his steadfast love
endures forever!"
Psalm 107:1

to aknowledge _____

I feel

The best part of my day

_____
_____
_____
_____
_____
_____
_____
_____

My worries

_____
_____
_____
_____
_____

Dear God, ♡

I am thankful for

_____
_____
_____
_____
_____
_____
_____
_____

I am praying for

_____
_____
_____
_____
_____
_____
_____
_____

to do

Today I learned a lot and I will practice

_____

_____

_____

_____

Thank you, God, for listening to me!

to doodle

Amen

"But the Lord is faithful.
He will establish you and
guard you against the evil one."
2 Thessalonians 3:3

to aknowledge _____

I feel

The best part of my day

_____
_____
_____
_____
_____
_____
_____
_____

My worries

_____
_____
_____
_____

to write

Dear God, ♡

I am thankful for

_____
_____
_____
_____
_____
_____
_____
_____

I am praying for

_____
_____
_____
_____
_____
_____
_____
_____

to do

Today I learned a lot and I will practice

Thank you, God, for listening to me!

to doodle

Amen

"And as you wish
that others
would do to you,
do so to them."
Luke 6:31

to aknowledge

I feel

The best part of my day

_____
_____
_____
_____
_____
_____
_____
_____

My worries

_____
_____
_____
_____

to write

Dear God, ♡

I am thankful for

_____
_____
_____
_____
_____
_____
_____
_____

I am praying for

_____
_____
_____
_____
_____
_____
_____
_____

to do

Today I learned a lot and I will practice

_____

_____

_____

_____

_____

Thank you, God, for listening to me!

to doodle

Amen

"Peace I leave with you;
my peace I give to you.
Not as the world gives
do I give to you.
Let not your hearts be troubled,
neither let them be afraid."
John 14:27

to aknowledge

I feel

The best part of my day

_____
_____
_____
_____
_____
_____
_____

My worries

_____
_____
_____
_____
_____
_____

Dear God, ♡

I am thankful for

_____
_____
_____
_____
_____
_____
_____

I am praying for

_____
_____
_____
_____
_____
_____
_____
_____

to do

Today I learned a lot and I will practice

_____

_____

_____

_____

_____

Thank you, God, for listening to me!

to doodle

Amen

"I give you thanks, O LORD,
with my whole heart;
before the gods,
I sing your praise."
Psalm 138:1

to aknowledge

I feel

The best part of my day

_____
_____
_____
_____
_____
_____
_____
_____
_____

My worries

_____
_____
_____
_____
_____

to write

Dear God, ♡

I am thankful for

_____
_____
_____
_____
_____
_____
_____
_____
_____

I am praying for

_____
_____
_____
_____
_____
_____
_____
_____
_____

to do

Today I learned a lot and I will practice

_____

_____

_____

_____

_____

Thank you, God, for listening to me!

to doodle

Amen

"Be kind to one another,
tenderhearted, forgiving
one another,
as God in Christ forgave you."
Ephesians 4:32

to aknowledge

I feel

The best part of my day

My worries

to write

Dear God, ♡

I am thankful for

_____

_____

_____

_____

_____

_____

_____

I am praying for

_____

_____

_____

_____

_____

_____

_____

to do

Today I learned a lot and I will practice

_____

_____

_____

_____

Thank you, God, for listening to me!

to doodle

Amen

to read

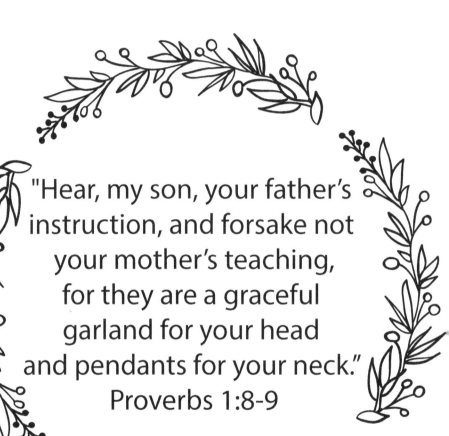

"Hear, my son, your father's
instruction, and forsake not
your mother's teaching,
for they are a graceful
garland for your head
and pendants for your neck."
Proverbs 1:8-9

to aknowledge

I feel

😃 😊 😐 ☹️ 😞

The best part of my day

_____
_____
_____
_____
_____
_____
_____
_____

My worries

_____
_____
_____
_____

to write

Dear God, ♡

I am thankful for

_____

_____

_____

_____

_____

_____

_____

_____

_____

I am praying for

_____

_____

_____

_____

_____

_____

_____

_____

to do

Today I learned a lot and I will practice

_____

_____

_____

_____

Thank you, God, for listening to me!

to doodle

Amen

"And whatever you ask
in prayer, you will receive,
if you have faith."
Matthew 21:22

to aknowledge

I feel

The best part of my day

_____

_____

_____

_____

_____

_____

_____

My worries

_____

_____

_____

_____

Dear God, ♡

I am thankful for

_____
_____
_____
_____
_____
_____
_____
_____
_____

I am praying for

_____
_____
_____
_____
_____
_____
_____
_____
_____

to do

Today I learned a lot and I will practice

_____

_____

_____

_____

Thank you, God, for listening to me!

to doodle

Amen

"Jesus Christ is the same yesterday, today and forever."
Hebrews 13:8

to aknowledge

I feel

The best part of my day

_____
_____
_____
_____
_____
_____
_____
_____

My worries

_____
_____
_____
_____

to write

Dear God, ♡

I am thankful for

_____
_____
_____
_____
_____
_____
_____
_____

I am praying for

_____
_____
_____
_____
_____
_____
_____
_____

to do

Today I learned a lot and I will practice

Thank you, God, for listening to me!

to doodle

Amen

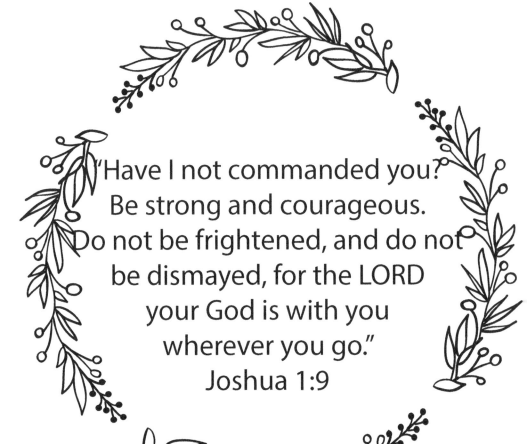

"Have I not commanded you?
Be strong and courageous.
Do not be frightened, and do not
be dismayed, for the LORD
your God is with you
wherever you go."
Joshua 1:9

to aknowledge

I feel

The best part of my day

_____
_____
_____
_____
_____
_____
_____
_____

My worries

_____
_____
_____
_____
_____

to write

Dear God, ♡

I am thankful for

_____
_____
_____
_____
_____
_____
_____
_____

I am praying for

_____
_____
_____
_____
_____
_____
_____
_____
_____

to do

Today I learned a lot and I will practice

_____

_____

_____

_____

_____

Thank you, God, for listening to me!

to doodle

Amen

"The LORD bless you
and keep you;"
Numbers 6:24

to aknowledge _____

I feel

The best part of my day

_____
_____
_____
_____
_____
_____
_____

My worries

_____
_____
_____
_____

to write

Dear God, ♡

I am thankful for

_____
_____
_____
_____
_____
_____
_____
_____

I am praying for

_____
_____
_____
_____
_____
_____
_____
_____

to do

Today I learned a lot and I will practice

Thank you, God, for listening to me!

to doodle

Amen

Thank you for your purchase and we hope you enjoyed our book!

Your feedback is greatly appreciated as it lets us know how we are doing!

For all inquiries, email us at rosetrifoliapress@gmail.com

Rose Trifolia Press

Made in the USA
Middletown, DE
24 June 2022